URBAN GARDENING
AND FARMING
FOR TEENS™

COMMUNITY GARDENS

GROW YOUR OWN VEGETABLES AND HERBS

SUSAN BURNS CHONG

ROSEN
PUBLISHING®

New York

This book is dedicated to my great and courageous family.

Published in 2014 by The Rosen Publishing Group, Inc.
29 East 21st Street, New York, NY 10010

First Edition

Library of Congress Cataloging-in-Publication Data

Chong, Susan Burns, author.
Community gardens: grow your own vegetables and herbs/Susan Burns Chong.
     pages cm.—(Urban gardening and farming for teens)
Includes bibliographical references and index.
ISBN 978-1-4777-1777-6 (library binding)
1. Community gardens—Juvenile literature. 2. Gardening for teenagers—Juvenile literature. 3. Vegetable gardening—Juvenile literature. I. Title.
SB457.3.C47 2014
635.09173'2—dc23

2013014170

Manufactured in the United States of America

CPSIA Compliance Information: Batch #W14YA: For further information, contact Rosen Publishing, New York, New York, at 1-800-237-9932.

Contents

Introduction

In Youngstown, Ohio, a group of teens has built a large community garden. They hope to end hunger in their town. "We want to get the community involved and plan on using the garden to benefit others," said participant Jordan Hirschhaut in an interview with the *Tribune Chronicle*. They will tend their garden with residents of a nursing home. Food will be donated for cooking classes. Produce will be sold at the nearby farmers' market. The harvest will be shared among the people working together.

If you are also thinking about community gardening, you are not alone. You will be joining a nationwide movement of new gardeners. Teens are grabbing shovels, donning work gloves, and pulling on boots. They are starting to garden. They are growing herbs and vegetables on windowsills, rooftops, vacant lots, the grounds of schools and social service agencies, and local farms.

Growing food can teach people young and old about taking care of planet Earth. As scientists learn more about our planet, the public better understands the fragile balance of nature. People see the importance of taking care of Earth's soil, water, air, and living things. These are our natural resources.

Gardening can even teach us about caring for our bodies. Food purchased at stores and restaurants can contain all kinds of ingredients that may be harmful. People who want to be healthy choose fresh food instead.

Teens in Athens, Georgia, work in a community garden. The produce they grow is sold at a local farmers' market. The money they raise benefits older people living in their city.

However, many families in the United States cannot afford to eat fresh food. In 2011, the U.S. Department of Agriculture (USDA) published a report about food security. Food security means that families have enough food for healthy, active living. According to the report, eighteen million American families did not have food security. Last year, community gardeners donated thousands of pounds (kilograms) of produce to needy families.

Community gardening teaches life and job skills, too. People learn patience, persistence, and problem solving. These come in handy in the workplace. Teens are earning job experience and money through community gardens. Plus, planting, weeding, and harvesting can be a real workout!

Most important, community gardens bring people together. Gardeners can have different ages, ethnicities, spiritual beliefs, and cultural backgrounds. By working together in the garden, valuable friendships are made, and the community gets stronger.

CHAPTER ONE

WHAT IS COMMUNITY GARDENING?

In a community garden, you get to work together and share resources. According to the American Community Gardening Association (ACGA), about eighteen thousand community gardens are tended each year in the United States and Canada. Each garden is unique. The participants bring their own ideas, culture, and preferences to their work on the land. These influences are reflected in the gardens themselves.

People create community gardens for many reasons. Some gardens are designed to teach neighbors about nutritional science, cooking, and healthy eating. Other gardens are made for people to grow food for themselves or their families. Some gardens teach job skills and allow participants to earn money. Sometimes gardens assist low-income people by giving away fresh food. Many gardens provide a quiet meeting place in a busy neighborhood. Some offer a wildlife habitat in an urban setting. In some communities, gardeners just need to garden!

Gardeners often share their wisdom, hoping to create a new generation of younger gardening enthusiasts.

GARDEN CROPS

Nationwide, community gardens are producing hundreds of thousands of pounds (kilograms) of fresh produce. Knowing more about food plants can help gardeners think about what to grow in their gardens. Almost all plants have six edible parts: roots, stems, leaves, flowers, fruits, and seeds. (Of course, gardeners must check before eating. Not all parts of all plants are edible.)

Vegetables that grow underground are called root crops. These include sweet potatoes, turnips, radishes, and garlic. Stem crops,

Gardeners at the Eastwind Community Garden in Marina Del Rey, California, grow leafy crops, such as chard, kale, and lettuce, in raised beds.

such as leeks, celery, and kohlrabi, are well known for their sturdy, healthy stems. Plants such as kale, cabbage, spinach, and lettuce are called leafy crops and are famous for their big, leafy appearance.

When eating broccoli, cauliflower, and nasturtium, we are actually eating flowers! These are called flower crops. Fruit crops include more than apples, strawberries, and grapes. The fruit of a plant includes produce such as tomatoes, bean pods, and corn kernels. Peas, wheat, sunflowers, and lima beans are known as seed crops.

Good cooks know the value of herbs in the kitchen. Some herbs are perennials. These are plants that return season after season. Catnip, bee balm, and chives are examples. Other herbs are annuals. These are plants that need to be planted newly each year. Cilantro, basil, and parsley are types of annuals.

LEARNING FROM EXPERIENCE

Gardeners love to learn from each other. Take time to share ideas and stories about what has worked and what has not. You will be surprised by what you learn. A garden project in Vancouver, Washington, has a formal mentoring program. New gardeners are matched with lifelong gardeners. Even if you don't have a mentoring program, you can find tons of specific gardening advice for your region. Your local hardware, feed, or garden store, the library, and online sources are all places to explore.

Community gardeners often plant herbs. Herbs can help ward off pesky insects or animals. They are rumored to improve the taste of vegetables planted nearby. Some herbs, such as anise hyssop and lemon balm, can even be medicinal, curing everything from muscle aches to sore throats. Visit your local food store or farmers' market to become familiar with the diversity of vegetables and herbs available.

GARDEN LOCATION AND DESIGN

Community gardens may be located on public or private land. This land may be rented, leased, borrowed, or owned. Sites may

Friendships are an important part of community gardening. These two friends in the Dorchester neighborhood of Boston, Massachusetts, water their own garden plot and help their neighbors' plants, too.

include vacant lots in a city, or land on college and university campuses. Many schools, churches, synagogues, mosques, hospitals, and social service agencies lend land for garden projects. If they lack access to land, community gardeners can be creative and grow gardens on windowsills and rooftops.

The overall design of the community garden may be either communal or divided. A communal garden allows for one large plot. This plot is tended and harvested by the entire group. A divided, or allotment, garden is designed for multiple individuals, families, or groups. They work their own smaller plots of land.

Additional considerations for the community garden come from the gardeners themselves. If the garden will engage very young children, gardeners often add clearly marked paths or small places to play. If the members are mostly older people, raised-bed gardens may be easier to tend. Benches can provide a resting place for tired gardeners. The Americans with Disabilities Act (ADA) offers further recommendations for making public spaces accessible to people with disabilities.

ORGANIZATIONAL STRUCTURE

Good leadership is important for the success and sustainability of a community gardening project. A small committee of gardeners usually takes charge of the project. The leadership team gathers ideas from the larger group of volunteers. The landowner may also participate. The city, town, church, synagogue, school, or social service agency hosting the garden may also get involved. Sometimes the host institution has oversight of the project.

SAFETY IN THE GARDEN

While most parts of the plants you grow are edible, remember to find out before you chew on something. For example, rhubarb stems are delicious baked in a strawberry pie. Beware! The pretty red and green leaves are poisonous to people and pets. Raw lima beans, peach pits, and foliage on cherry trees are all dangerous to eat. Learn more online about poisonous vegetation. In addition to looking out for scary plant parts, don't forget to be prepared. Wear your sun hat, garden gloves, sunscreen, and bug repellant when you are working outside.

Remember to take good care of yourself while you are in the garden. Help your friends be careful, too. Take breaks and drink plenty of water when you are in the hot sun.

Many of the resources available in community gardens, such as tools, water, seeds, and soil, are donated locally. They may also be funded through federal, state, or local grants. To help protect these resources, the leadership team may create strict rules for gardeners to follow. These rules cover issues such as sharing donated supplies, helping with maintenance, or conserving water.

The leadership team also draws on each member's strengths and talents. For example, one member may send out a garden newsletter, tweets, or e-mails. Another may be skilled at leading work crews or recruiting new members. Everyone has an important role to play in the community gardening project.

CHAPTER TWO

GETTING INVOLVED

If you are ready to get involved in community gardening, you have choices. You might join a garden that is in your neighborhood or at your school. You might join by yourself or with family or friends. If you do not have one nearby, you may find that you need to start your own garden.

Creating a new garden can be both challenging and rewarding. In Wilton, Connecticut, seventeen-year-old Karina Olsen started a community garden in her neighborhood. She wrote a grant proposal and worked with the teen center and the YMCA. She asked stores for donations. Karina invited friends, family, and neighbors to break ground for the garden. It was a lot of work. She told the local newspaper, the *Wilton Villager*, "Seeing it come together is great."

JOIN AN EXISTING GARDEN

You can learn about community garden projects in your town by talking with neighbors, friends, storeowners, and teachers.

A mother and her daughters work together in a raised-bed garden in Sherwood, Oregon. The local church transformed its front yard into a community garden.

The Bi-National Community Garden Database, at http://acga .localharvest.org, is also helpful for finding registered gardens close to your home. The database includes gardens in both the United States and Canada.

When joining a garden, teens often invite family members to assist them. Sometimes they ask people with gardening experience for help. They may invite friends from school or community groups.

Community gardens have rules about maintaining the garden plots. If you are working alone, you should be prepared to visit the garden every day. If you are working as a group or family, you should be ready to share the responsibilities.

Usually, organizations charge a fee for the garden plots. Often they will allow gardeners to contribute a service to the garden program in exchange for the fee. Helping with chores, getting donations, or leading an event are examples of volunteer work.

START YOUR OWN GARDEN

Whether you live in the country, the city, or the suburbs, you can start your own community garden. These are a few steps to follow.

First, you must get excited about the project. Then, you need to energize other people. Starting with important stakeholders, such as friends, neighbors, neighborhood association members, and community leaders, you explore the idea. Then, you host community meetings. At these meetings, the group brainstorms ideas and develops goals for the garden. The group may also define rules and build a strategy for getting resources.

When community garden projects begin, many different stakeholders are involved. They may have a lot, a little, or no experience working as a group. The members may not always agree with each other. Having discussions and making decisions may be challenging at first. Leaders must be ready to have both difficult and joyful moments.

Leaders help participants set ground rules about how the group will work together. These rules may include ideas such as showing respect, taking turns, sharing ideas, or coming with an open mind. Setting an agenda is important, too. People who come to meetings want to know the kinds of decisions that will be made. Leaders or a small group may set the agenda.

Notetaker and timekeeper are two important roles to fill at every meeting. Notetakers write down notes about the discussion

WINDOW FARMING

Window farms are a great idea if you do not have access to land. As long as you have a sunny window, you can grow your own edibles. In some cities, people have worked together to make window farms. They bring recycled bottles, tubing, and seeds to grow. No soil is needed! You can learn more about this hydroponic system of growing herbs and vegetables at http://www.windowfarms.com.

and jot down action steps. Timekeepers ensure that the meeting starts and ends on time. They also make sure that the group follows the agenda.

As the project moves forward, partners should be invited to participate. Partners may bring valuable resources. For example, natural or elected community leaders can help with access to land or volunteers. Business leaders may donate tools or supplies, and philanthropists may donate money. Master gardeners can give good advice about gardening in your area and volunteer their time.

GARDENING RESOURCES

Community gardening uses natural resources such as dirt, sun, and rain. Still, you will need money to get started. Tools, supplies, and equipment can be expensive. Hand trowels, rakes, pruning shears, and pitchforks are a must. Mulch, soil, and path materials are necessary supplies. Rain barrels, compost bins, and storage units are recommended, too.

Tools like these are essential for gardening. Consider asking friends and family to lend their tools. Check out Habitat for Humanity's ReStore or other household consignment shops, too.

Urban Harvest, an organization based in Houston, Texas, estimates that the cost of starting a new community garden could range from $1,500 to $4,000. The cost depends on the availability of water and the garden's size and design. Larger gardens on public land may cost more.

Establishing a garden may cost less with the help of donations. Money is available. At the local level, new gardeners can talk with area businesses and organizations. At the state level, teens can seek funding from community development grants or health initiatives. Nationally, public and private funders are willing to give money for new community gardens. A number of the organizations in the For More Information section can help with finding grants.

IMPORTANT CONSIDERATIONS

Members of a new community garden may face obstacles. They may need to work out details with the city or the landowner. If help is needed to solve problems, the local cooperative extension office and the ACGA can give advice. They can also advocate for your project.

Finding the right space to garden is important. The land must get at least six hours of sun a day. The site must be accessible

Volunteers in Camden, New Jersey, work to transform their city by creating new growing spaces. Cities that face high crime and poverty rates benefit greatly from community gardens.

by foot, bicycle, or car. The garden design must be community-friendly. The soil should be healthy.

Healthy soil can be challenging to find in the city. Land that has been used before may have tightly compacted soil. The soil may lack nutrients and may even be polluted. Paint, petroleum spills, sewage sludge, and fires are a few things that may lead to soil contamination. Common contaminants, according to the Environmental Protection Agency (EPA), include lead, cadmium, arsenic, zinc, and polycyclic aromatic hydrocarbons (PAHs).

Gardeners should find out about the health of the soil before digging. State and local environmental agencies and the local cooperative extension office can help you learn about the history of a site and do soil testing.

Do not give up if you cannot find healthy soil. If needed, gardeners can amend the soil, improving its quality by adding nutrients and organic matter. If the soil is contaminated, the EPA has several recommendations. Gardeners should use raised beds or containers with new, clean soil. They should also cover the pathways of gardens with grass, wood mulch, stone, or other materials. This is important, since contaminants can travel in the air or in rain splashes.

CHAPTER THREE

PLANNING YOUR GARDEN

Planning your garden takes creativity, ingenuity, and a little knowledge about your corner of the world. Gardeners make decisions based on what they know. They may ask questions like, "How much sun, shade, or rain does this area get?" Or, "What kinds of vegetables grow best here?" Or, "How long is the growing season?" Gardening in the mountains, deserts, plains, and coastal areas brings different challenges and opportunities. A community garden plot in Phoenix, Arizona, will look quite different from a plot in Montreal, Canada, or Charleston, South Carolina.

THE GEOGRAPHY OF GARDENING

Agriculturalists have studied the regional differences in growing plants throughout the United States and Canada for years. They started creating maps to illustrate these differences in the mid-1960s. With improved technology, more knowledge about the lives of plants, and a greater understanding of climate change,

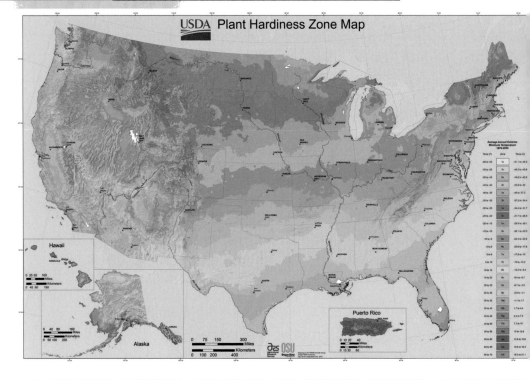

USDA Plant Hardiness Zone Map

The USDA Plant Hardiness Zone Map is a helpful tool. By using the map, gardeners can identify the plants that grow best in their regions.

the maps have changed. Gardeners may find these maps online at the American Horticultural Society (AHS) and USDA Web sites. Relevant maps may also be included on seed packets.

The USDA Plant Hardiness Zone Map helps gardeners predict which vegetables, flowers, shrubs, or trees may thrive in their areas. On the map, North America is divided into colored-coded zones. The different colors highlight how cold each area will get in the winter. Each section shows a 10°F (12°C) difference. Gardeners are then able to match their zone to the zones recommended for various plants. For example, a gardener in Maine wants to grow an orange tree outdoors. By using the map, she would see that she lives in Zone 5. The orange tree, recommended for Zone 9, would not be successful in Maine. It is too cold.

The American Horticultural Society's Heat Zone Map illustrates the number of days that plants will endure each year. "Hot" is defined as 86°F (30°C) or higher. By knowing the temperature range in the area, gardeners are better able to choose plants that will thrive. For example, a gardener in New Mexico needs to choose more heat-tolerant plants. He could grow vegetables like collard greens, cowpeas, or certain types of tomatoes.

The Old Farmer's Almanac estimates and lists the last spring and first fall frost dates for cities in the United States and Canada. Frost can damage new plants. By estimating the last day of frost in the spring, gardeners can make the most of the early season for direct sow planting. Frost can also damage crops. Predicting the first date of frost in fall allows gardeners to bring inside or cover less hardy plants to protect them.

ADDITIONAL SITE CONSIDERATIONS

Gardeners have even more to think about when planning their gardens. Sun, wind, and drainage are important to consider. Many crops, such as tomatoes or peas, need full or partial sun during the day. Some plants may need protection from wind in the garden site. Gardens along the coast, for example, are at risk for damaging winds. Gardeners can grow protective bushes or install fencing or walls to protect young plants. Drainage describes how rainwater flows from a garden. Poor drainage causes water puddles in a garden. This may hurt plants by making them vulnerable to disease.

Even if gardeners know their regions well, microclimates can be created. Natural or man-made elements can cause the climate of a small area to be unique. For example, in the city, asphalt, brick, or concrete can absorb heat from the sun. This raises the surrounding temperature, creating the need for heat-tolerant plants. Community garden beds that are on a hill or slope may make watering difficult. The water may run off instead of soaking into the soil. Further, the airflow down a slope may create frost pockets, or areas in which frost lingers, damaging plants. Observing microclimates is helpful for the next season's planning.

For gardeners living in areas with cold weather and short growing seasons, a cold frame allows for a longer season. The cold frame acts like a mini greenhouse for plants.

DESIGN IDEAS FOR PLANTING

Different garden designs solve problems that gardeners face. For example, with a space that is too small, gardeners can use square-foot gardening techniques. These allow plants to grow in areas measuring 1 foot by 1 foot (0.3 meter by 0.3 meter). This saves space, conserves water, and manages growth. Vertical gardening, or using structures that allow plants to grow up, not out, can also be helpful.

If the growing season is too short, a cold frame may do the trick. A cold frame is a wooden box with glass attached to the

In Avon, Colorado, volunteers prepare raised bed gardens. They chose to build high raised beds directly on the grassy turf. The group will fill in the boxes with fertile soil.

top. Gardeners often use windows to build this lid, which may be lowered, raised, or sealed closed. Using a cold frame can extend the growing season four to six weeks at each end. The danger in using a cold frame is not frost. It is dehydration and heat. The maximum temperature for plants should be about 75–80°F (24–27°C), so gardeners need to monitor the temperature and plan ways to prop up their lids.

A raised-bed design can solve many problems. For areas that are limited in size or have contaminated soil, raised beds are ideal. With the additional height, older adults or people in wheelchairs can enjoy gardening while seated. The design is basically a box frame with low or high sides, generally 3 to 5 feet (0.9 to 1.5 m) wide. This box is filled with a mix of good soil, manure, and compost.

GARDENS WITH A THEME

For a creative twist, gardeners can use a theme to plan their gardens. One idea is a favorite recipe garden. For example, gardeners who love salsa might plant tomatoes, hot peppers, onions, and cilantro. Gardeners who love pizza might plant tomatoes, green peppers, oregano, and basil. Other ideas might be soup, stir fry, or salad gardens. "Name gardens" are also becoming popular. These are gardens in which the names of the plants begin with letters that spell out the name of the gardener. One more idea is a therapy garden. Gardeners plant medicinal herbs, fragrant plants, or plants that attract wildlife. It is up to you!

With a shallow raised-bed design, preparing the soil under the area is a good idea for maximizing the success of the plot. Some gardeners recommend removing the grass or turf, turning the topsoil, and then adding the frame and the good mix. With a deep raised bed, gardeners can simply build the frame and fill in the good dirt. This design generally holds moisture longer than shallow plantings. In areas with contaminated soil, gardeners can place a layer of landscape fabric between the ground soil and clean soil. The fabric prevents the plants' roots from entering the ground soil under the bed.

Straw-bale gardening involves creating a straw-filled frame that is topped with soil. This allows for even taller garden plots. This design is helpful for people with arthritis and other physical ailments who prefer to stand.

Container gardening can address several concerns. If the space gets too much sun, shade, wind, or rain, containers can be moved. Containers can also work if the soil is contaminated. Containers may be clay, plastic, stone, cement, concrete, metal, or wood. Imagination is the limit. Containers are less susceptible to pests and weeds, too.

STRUCTURES IN YOUR GARDEN

A variety of structures may be used for making the most of your space or for giving support. These can be bought at a store or made by hand. Typical structures use wood, bamboo, metal, or fencing. Poles connected at the top, fencing attached as an A-frame, or wire in a cylindrical or circular shape may provide help for plants.

COMPANION PLANTING

Gardeners often plant specific vegetables together. The plants may help each other as they grow. One of the oldest known companion plantings is the "Three Sisters" method. This is a traditional practice of indigenous North American farmers. It involves growing squash, corn, and climbing beans together. This is how it works: The squash grows across the garden plot. Its leaves protect the tender young corn stalks and bean sprouts. As the corn grows taller, the beans have a sturdy stalk to climb. The beans then provide extra stability for the corn against windy weather.

Since most community garden plots are small, gardeners may grow plants vertically to save room for other plants. Using structures may allow for companion planting, too. Some plants need something to support them. Sugar snap peas and string beans love to climb. Even tomatoes benefit from having a little help, especially as the fruits grow heavier.

DRAFTING THE IDEAS

Gardeners are often dreamers. They need to keep track of ideas. Resources are available to help gardeners remember their plans. Gardeners recommend taking lots of photos from seed to harvest each year. Keeping notes on what worked or what failed helps them learn more about their practice. A garden journal or notebook works well for this. Seed company and garden store

Web sites provide free, downloadable garden calendars. Even iTunes offers several fun apps for gardeners, such as Garden Time Planner, Garden Tracker—Bumper Crop, and the Essential Garden Guide. They provide plant and species information, chore lists, design help, and games.

When drafting the design for the actual plot, gardeners must know the measurements of the area. Then, they make predictions about the size and shape that the plants will become. Garden books and seed packets can help with dimensions. Gardeners can even sketch what the plot will look like during different times of the growing season.

CHAPTER FOUR

PREPARING AND PLANTING

Now that you have done the hard work of planning your garden plot, you are ready to get dirty. For some gardeners, this is the part that brings the most satisfaction. "I was just so happy putting my hands in the ground, being around people who also liked putting their hands in the ground," wrote a Youth Harvest participant from Missoula, Montana. To create the best environment for plants to grow, get to know your soil and what your seeds need to thrive in it.

SOIL

Healthy soil is vitally important to the success of your garden. If your soil has the right mix of nutrients and drainage, you will be heading in the right direction. How do you find out about your soil? How do you discover what your soil needs?

By understanding plant nutrition, gardeners can best provide for plants. Plants need sixteen naturally occurring elements to thrive. Three nonmineral elements are found in the air and water.

SOIL PH

You have probably learned a little about pH in your science class. The pH level is important to plants because it determines how plants access the trace elements in the soil. The results from a soil test can inform gardeners about their soil. When the soil is low on the pH scale (1.0), it is more acidic. When it is higher on the scale (14.0), it is more alkaline. While most plants prefer soil that is in the middle of the pH scale (7.0), some plants need soil that is more specific. Gardeners can play around with the soil's pH level. They can add organic matter to change the level. If the pH is too high, gardeners may add sawdust, peat moss, or pine needles to increase acidity. If the pH is too low, some plants may be in danger, and gardeners may add limestone or wood ash.

These are hydrogen, oxygen, and carbon. With the help of the sun's energy, they create food for plants through photosynthesis.

The remaining thirteen elements are minerals. They are found in soil. They include both macronutrients and micronutrients. The primary macronutrients for a plant's well-being are nitrogen, phosphorus, and potassium. The secondary macronutrients are calcium, magnesium, and sulfur. The remaining seven elements are the micronutrients. Boron, copper, iron, chloride, manganese, molybdenum, and zinc are needed in trace amounts.

Since it is impossible to know what elements are in the soil by looking at the garden plot, gardeners test the soil. Soil tests can be done through local cooperative extension offices. Gardeners can also buy soil tests at the local hardware store to do themselves. The results from soil tests will give clues about what the soil needs to be more productive. The missing elements may then be added to the soil.

Healthy soil has not only all thirteen minerals but also good drainage and density. "Loam" is the word that describes the right balance of sand, silt, and clay. A handful of loam can be rolled into a smooth ball and is not sticky to the touch. Most garden plots, however, have too much clay or too much sand.

Gardeners know they have too much clay if their soil retains water, even during a dry period with little rain. Also, a handful of heavy clay soil can be rolled into a ball, leaving hands sticky. With the addition of compost, the soil will allow roots to develop, and with more sand, the drainage will improve.

Sandy soil is easy to work with, but does not hold water well. Nutrients often get washed out. A handful of sandy soil crumbles and cannot be rolled into a ball. With the addition of a cover crop, such as clover, buckwheat, or soybeans, sandy soils can improve.

This process of adding materials, such as compost, manure, lime, peat moss, sand, and gravel, to change the soil is called amending the soil.

SEEDS

When gardeners plan their crops, they look to the seed packets for guidance. Seed packets describe where, when, and how to sow the seed. They detail the amount of sun or shade needed. They may also include spacing, known as isolation distances, and the number of days before the harvest. Packets even recommend the calendar month in which to plant outdoors.

For every plant, there is a defined germination period in which the seed begins to grow. Gardeners must determine how to plant

Seed packets are sold at most hardware, feed, and garden stores and online. Read the directions carefully and be sure to buy seeds that can be grown in your region.

the seed. Seeds can be sown directly in the soil or given a head start and raised as indoor seedlings first. Carrots and parsnips, for example, do not like to have their roots disturbed, so their seeds must be sown directly in the ground. Tomato and pea plants, on the other hand, fare much better when grown indoors first. They are susceptible to pests when they are young. They can then be transplanted into the garden as seedlings.

DIRECT SOWING

When planting seeds that are directly sown outdoors, gardeners need to check the soil temperature first. Gardeners know if the soil is warm enough by using a soil thermometer. The

33

A gardener drops her bean seeds in a row. The green string, tied to small posts at each end of the row, helps her remember where she planted the seeds.

thermometer is placed in a hole about 5 to 6 inches (13 to 15 centimeters) deep. If the soil temperature measures 41°F (5°C), it may be safe enough for most seeds. However, more tender plants, like corn or green beans, require slightly warmer soil.

To prepare the soil for direct sowing, gardeners will need water, a rake, and a hand trowel. First, gardeners rake and wet the soil. Next, they use a hand trowel, or small hand shovel, to make the row at the required depth. Next, the seeds are dropped into the soil along the row. Soil is pushed back over the row, covering the seeds.

When organized rows are not essential, broadcasting is another great way to get seeds into the dirt. Gardeners basically toss seeds onto soil that has been prepared. They then rake over the area, lightly covering seeds with soil. Seed tape is another method, in which seeds are attached to a biodegradable strip that is planted in the soil. Again, seed packets provide excellent directions to help determine which method to utilize.

GROWING SEEDLINGS

Some plants do best when grown indoors first and transplanted, or moved from one place to another. To get started, gardeners rely on small containers, soil, a light source, a watering can, and, of course, seeds.

Garden stores offer a variety of containers at a range of prices. Seasoned gardeners often creatively recycle to save money. They use old food containers, egg cartons, or boxes for planting. Some gardeners even make their own pots using newspaper. They wrap the paper around a cup or a bowl, about the desired size of the

Teens are active in a new community garden in Brooklyn, New York. Here, they examine their seedlings closely before planting them.

pot. The gardener tapes the side and the bottom and removes it from the object. A new biodegradable planter is created!

Garden stores sell large trays for seedlings. These trays come with clear plastic lids. The lids help create a greenhouse effect, raising the temperature and keeping moisture inside. For gardeners with only a small space to use, recycled lids or plastic bags may cover individual plants.

Some plants benefit from hardening off, or getting used to being outside before being planted. Plants are placed outside for several hours during the day. Then they return to the greenhouse at night, often with reduced watering. When they are ready, they are planted outdoors.

PROTECTING ENDANGERED PLANTS

Maine's Medomak Valley High School students are on a mission. Students at the high school save heirloom seeds. They want to preserve the genetic diversity of plants. Heirloom seeds are ones that are no longer cultivated on larger, commercial farms. Students focus on growing vegetables and fruits that are part of history. The plants may be connected with tribal communities or may have been threatened by the growth of cities. Students grow the plants, save the seeds, and then share them with other gardeners.

Any soil can be used for starting seedlings. A sowing mix, multipurpose potting mix, or peat-free soil mix is most promising. Garden store staff members know what to recommend.

TRANSPLANTING

Community gardeners may choose to buy seedlings from the local nursery, garden club, or hardware store. They may want just one or two plants of a particular type. Sometimes the appropriate time has passed by without starting the seed indoors. Sometimes the attempt to grow the seed has failed. (It happens!) Whatever the reason, when buying seedlings, gardeners check for signs of healthy plants. These signs include strong stems, bushy green leaves, and healthy roots. Gardeners always ask for directions about where, when, and how to plant the seedlings. Seedlings require careful handling and a heavy soaking when they are first planted.

LABELING YOUR PLANTS

Gardeners know the importance of labeling the rows when planting seeds or seedlings. Baby plants look similar. Areas of broadcasted seeds are almost impossible to identify.

Garden stores offer many expensive and inexpensive options when it comes to labeling rows. Wood, copper, and metal signs can beautifully display the names of herbs and vegetables. For cheaper, do-it-yourself options, gardeners can use a variety of free or recycled materials. Wooden paint stirrers, free at most hardware stores, make great signs. Painted rocks or shells also work. Even strips from old window blinds with lettering in permanent marker make durable signs. Some gardeners attach the seed packet, covered in a plastic bag, to popsicle sticks or branches. They place them at the head of each row.

It is important to note that some plants can spread their root systems throughout a garden. This creates competition with other plants for water, sun, and nutrients. Herbs in the mint family, such as peppermint and bee balm, are examples. Strawberries can be a challenge, too. These and others should be planted in containers or in a separate plot.

CHAPTER FIVE

TENDING YOUR GARDEN

Now that you have done the incredible work of planning and planting, the daily work of gardening begins. This requires patience and attention. You can probably tell how your friends are doing when you see them in the hallway. You know when they are tired, hungry, or happy. In the same way, during your daily visits to the garden, you will begin to notice how your plants are faring.

WATERING YOUR PLANTS

In community gardens, watering plants can be a challenge. Gardeners may need to bring in their own water in large watering cans, buckets, or gallon jugs. Many gardens have water pumps or wells on site. Some gardens have faucets on site. Plastic rain barrels are a popular way to collect rainwater. Often, local sanitation departments will offer rain barrels at a reduced cost.

If the community garden has a water source, hoses may be used. Gardeners may use a variety of different methods for watering. Handheld sprayers may send out a large amount of

The first time this gardener watered her plants, she calculated the number of minutes it took to get the soil wet at least 6 inches (15 cm) deep.

water to plants and their leaves. Sprinklers placed on the ground may water plants for a longer time. These can be more energy-efficient when used with a timer. Timers limit the amount of water used. Soaker hoses are positioned on the ground, winding around plants, and allow water to seep directly into the soil.

Gardeners have a few tips for giving plants enough to drink. First, they recommend watering until the soil is wet around the roots. The soil should be saturated to a minimum depth of 6 inches (15 cm). Gardeners observe how long it takes to achieve water deep down. They use that amount of time as a gauge for the next watering. If the leaves continuously get wet, the plants may be vulnerable to diseases. Gardeners also suggest that watering during the early morning or early

CHANGING SEASONS

Plants seem to know when the seasons are changing. Plants have phytochromes, pigments that allow them to measure the amount of sun they receive in twenty-four hours. The phytochromes trigger the release of hormones, or growth factors, that make the plant do something, such as bloom, form a bulb, grow leaves, or drop leaves.

evening is best. This way, the water is less likely to evaporate before it can provide for the plants.

WEEDING AND FEEDING

A very important tip for new gardeners is to get the weeds out of the garden. Weeds steal water and nutrients from the desired vegetables and herbs.

Simply pulling on the weeds' leaves is not enough. Many gardeners advise that the most important weeding technique is taking out the plant's root. Two tools, the hoe and hand fork, are made for churning the soil and exposing the roots of weeds.

However, there are other helpful techniques to use. Weeds with flowers can look pretty, but they are producing seeds for more weeds! Dandelion, pigweed, and goosefoot are examples. By paying attention to these plants, gardeners can prevent more weeds from growing. A nonchemical approach to getting rid of weeds involves boiling water or strong vinegar. The weed will die when gardeners pour either on the base of the weed. Just be careful not to apply this treatment to good plants.

Weeding is an important part of working a plot in the community garden. Sometimes gardeners help each other remove weeds or spread mulch to prevent them.

To prevent weeds, mulching may be helpful. Gardeners may spread a variety of inorganic and organic materials over the surface of the soil. Inorganic mulch ideas, such as felt, newspaper, and plastic, may work. Organic mulch ideas, such as pine needles, bark, or straw, may help, too. Mulch may be added at any time of the year, and should be applied 2 to 4 inches (5 to 10 cm) thick.

Some gardeners recommend feeding plants with chemical fertilizer. Community gardens may have strict rules about their use, however. Chemicals can be harmful for people and pets. Over time, fertilizers can actually take the nutrients out of the soil. They may also leach and get into waterways.

Alternatives exist that are better for the environment. Gardeners can use only natural fertilizers. Adding organic materials , such as

THE LEARNING GARDEN

The Learning Garden, located in Venice, California, is one of the largest community gardens in the country. Since 2001, high school students have worked the 60,000 square foot (5,574 square meter) garden. They have grown organic vegetables and medicinal herbs. Students participate in classes focused on improving health. These cover topics such as martial arts, yoga, and cooking. These classes happen right in the garden! Many volunteers help each year. They come from nearby universities and the neighborhood. They help teach and tend the waterfall, pond, and the native California plant garden, which includes cacti and succulents.

This garden started as a small school-based project. Now many community volunteers, neighbors, and students dedicate hundreds of hours of service to the garden, working and learning together.

manure and compost, to the soil reduces the need for fertilizer. New gardeners can learn from experienced ones about local solutions for keeping soil healthy.

WILDLIFE AND PEST MANAGEMENT

The garden is a lively resource for humans. It also serves as a vital habitat for native wildlife. Gardeners often include plants that may attract wildlife. In the middle of the city, community gardens may be a welcome place for animals, birds, and insects. Gardeners look for ladybugs, ground beetles, bumblebees, honeybees, and praying mantises. Toads, bats, butterflies, and hummingbirds may also visit the garden. Animals and insects help pollinate the garden and eat unwanted pests.

Unfortunately, wildlife can be hungry! Rabbits, deer, chipmunks, and groundhogs may munch through a garden. Japanese beetles, squash bugs, ants, cabbage moths, and aphids may also plague the garden. By utilizing an integrated pest management approach, gardeners can rebalance the ecosystem. Chemical or chemical-free pesticides, natural predators, and garden design are part of this approach.

Experienced gardeners have creative solutions for controlling pests. They diversify plants, or grow more than one kind of plant. Pests that are attracted to a plant may eat that one but leave the rest alone. Many gardeners strategically place certain herbs, flowers, or vegetables near each other. Examples include planting basil near tomatoes to repel the hornworm and radishes near cucumbers to repel the squash bug. Attracting predators that eat pests can be helpful, too. Putting a water source in a garden attracts frogs, which eat garden-destroying slugs. Gardeners have lots of tricks.

CHAPTER SIX

HARVESTING YOUR GARDEN AND PLANNING FOR NEXT YEAR

Y ou have worked hard all season, and now the fruits of your labor have arrived! In your community garden, you will watch the experienced gardeners harvest their produce. Remember to think about what you have planted in your garden. Check your notes to see how many days your vegetables and herbs will need to grow. Look at them to see if they are ripe or ready to pick. Remember, many people will be happy to help you.

Once you decide that your vegetables are ready, you can remove them from the stem. Check them over for blemishes, bruises, or diseases. If they look good, put them carefully in a basket or box to carry them out of the garden.

WHAT TO DO NEXT

Gardeners do not like to waste food or resources. After the harvest, even the plants are turned into compost. The possibilities are endless for making the most out of the produce from the community garden.

Get to know your vegetables and what they will look like when they are ripe. Handle them carefully. Be sure to wash and dry them before eating.

Food made with fresh vegetables and herbs is the joy of gardening. If too much is harvested at once, then storing the produce is the next step. Gardeners determine the most appropriate place to store each type of vegetable. For potatoes, it may be a cool, dark cabinet. For carrots, it may be the refrigerator.

Canning; pickling; making jams, jellies, or chutneys; freezing; and drying are all ways to preserve crops for the long term. Each of these methods requires unique tools and equipment. Everything must be extremely clean in the process, and the containers must be sterilized. This means they have to be free from any contaminants. The National Center for Home Food Preservation offers advice on how to can and store food safely.

Canning preserves food by sealing it in a container. Pickling involves preserving fruits or vegetables in vinegar. This makes them sweet, sour, spicy, or salty. Making jams requires cooking fruit, sugar, and butter for some time to specific temperatures. Jellies are similar to jams. These require straining the fruit for a smoother texture. Chutneys are made with chopped fruits and vegetables. Cooked with sugar, spices, and vinegar, they are then canned. Fruits, vegetables, and herbs can be dried in either the oven or the open air. Vegetables and fruits should be frozen quickly. Then they should be thawed slowly for the best results.

GARDENING ENTREPRENEURSHIP

Teens can be both gardeners and entrepreneurs. Around the country, young entrepreneurs are sprouting new small businesses from their gardens. Teens can earn money through gardening by selling fresh fruits and vegetables. Some teens use their harvest to create new products to sell. No matter the idea, having a business plan is very important. It includes information that will help guide business decisions. A business plan identifies the need for the product, the likely customers, costs, marketing strategies, and more.

Community gardeners may plan to sell their fresh produce. They can do this in a number of ways. Gardeners can sell their harvest on their own at a farm stand along the road. Gardeners who sell at larger farmers' markets may have more potential customers. Selling directly to restaurants or other businesses means guaranteed customers. Community supported agriculture (CSA) arrangements give gardeners money they can count on. CSAs allow people to pay at the beginning of the season for a weekly share of the harvest.

Entrepreneurs learn valuable life skills and earn money. Here, a young person sorts produce at a farm stand near Prairie View, Illinois.

Many groups of young gardeners have discovered how to turn their crops into what are called "value-added products." To create these, the produce is turned into something. A common example is turning maple sap into maple syrup or candies. Teens are creating and selling products like jarred spices, compost, dried gourds, candles, and more. In Rochester, New York, students involved in the Rochester Roots School-Community Garden Project are growing calendula and comfrey. They use these plants to make lip balms and skin salves. They sell their products at local businesses and online.

FARMERS' MARKETS SELLING LOCALLY

Working in a farmers' market can seem intimidating. Lori Phillips, a student at West Roxbury High School in Boston, sells produce with her school group. She recently told the magazine *Edible Boston* that working in the market changed her. "At first I didn't have a lot of confidence talking to people, but it built. People have reinforced it." According to the USDA, nearly eight thousand farmers' markets were open for business throughout America in 2011. Consumers spent an estimated $1.5 billion for fresh, local produce at these markets. The Farmers' Market Coalition can be a valuable resource for those interested in this field.

GARDENING PHILANTHROPY

Community gardens can be powerful classrooms. They can help people learn about nutrition, Earth, and food security. Garden groups often host workshops or events. They also take action. They make donations of produce, time, or money. The Plant a Row for the Hungry program is an example of an innovative idea from the Garden Writers Association and the GWA Foundation. Gardeners are encouraged to plant an extra row in their gardens. Then, they donate their extra harvest to hunger relief organizations. The Plant a Row program reports that in the past 18 years, gardeners have donated over 18 million pounds (over 8 million kilograms) of produce, creating 72 million meals.

Members of a community garden group near Toronto, Canada, gather together each week. They prepare meals with their fresh produce. These meals are donated to families in need.

Food banks, soup kitchens, and social service agencies distribute any donations to families in need. Gardening groups often volunteer time for gleaning at local farms. Gleaning is the practice of harvesting the crops that are healthy but do not look pretty enough to sell. These are then donated. Community garden groups may even donate a percentage of the profit from the sales at farmers' markets to hunger relief organizations.

PLANNING FOR NEXT YEAR

Gardeners know a valuable secret—the next season is another chance for success! If they have a bad harvest one year, they know that they will get another opportunity the following year.

CREATING GARDENS ABOVE THE CITY

Teens staying at Covenant House's homeless shelters are building rooftop gardens. They have planted gardens atop tall buildings in places like New York City, Washington, D.C., and Toronto, Canada. Environmental experts believe that rooftop gardens may have big benefits. They may help reduce the use of energy in buildings. They may even reduce the effects of pollution, especially in cities. These teens are not only learning a valuable skill for future careers in the green economy, but they are also helping the world.

Gardeners take the time between seasons to think and plan. Some even keep a journal with ideas, articles, or magazine clippings. By reviewing their notes and photos, they can be creative. Gardeners are always learning.

One strategy that gardeners suggest for a new season is called crop rotation. This is the practice of introducing new plants and moving the last year's crops around the garden. Vegetables and herbs get planted in new places with different companions. In this way, gardeners can reduce the risk of plant diseases and pests. Crop rotation also helps the soil. Growing the same plants year after year may deplete the soil's macronutrients and micronutrients. Changing the plants may replenish these nutrients.

Much like adding new plants to the plots, community gardens thrive when new gardeners are added. Community gardeners are always recruiting new people. Participants must communicate the importance of the garden project. They can do this through fund-raisers, campaigns, newsletters, and online updates. Community gardeners also recognize the generosity of the community. They take time to show their gratitude for donations. They write thank-you letters or give public recognition in newsletters, newspapers, or radio spots.

Hosting garden events is a great way to honor the work, thank supporters, and inspire new gardeners. Garden parties may include music, games, and conversation. They should also include fresh food from the garden.

Congratulations to you as you begin your journey into the rewarding and challenging world of gardening. In a community garden, you are never alone on the path. You will be surrounded by people who have learned from their elders. And they have learned from theirs. So please, enjoy the wisdom—and your dinner!

AGENDA A list of topics that the participants in a meeting will discuss.

AMEND To change and improve the composition of the soil.

ANNUAL A plant that needs to be planted anew each year.

BROADCASTING A method for planting seeds that involves tossing them onto the soil, rather than planting them in neat rows.

COMPOST BIN A container that holds organic materials, such as leaves, grass clippings, and food waste, that will be turned into compost.

COOPERATIVE EXTENSION A program run by local universities that supports gardening and agriculture.

DIRECT SOWING A method for planting seeds that requires tucking seeds directly into the soil, usually in rows at specific soil depths.

GERMINATION PERIOD The length of time that is required for a seed to begin growing.

GRANT Money that people apply for and may receive to support projects.

GROWING SEASON The time period between the last frost in spring and the first frost in fall.

HEAT TOLERANT Able to thrive in climates with many hot days.

HYDROPONIC SYSTEM A method of growing plants using sun, water, and nutrients but not soil.

ISOLATION DISTANCE The distance that gardeners should leave between seedlings during the planting process.

NURSERY A place where young plants are raised for sale and transplanting.

PERENNIAL A plant that returns each year, often increasing in size from the previous year.

PHILANTHROPIST A person who gives away money to help others, sometimes through grants.

STAKEHOLDER An important person or party that might be interested in or affected by a project.

SUSTAINABILITY The ability to keep something going for a long time without causing harm.

TRANSPLANT To uproot or remove a plant growing in one location and replant it in another.

TURNING The process of digging up the top layer of soil and remixing it into the plot.

FOR MORE INFORMATION

American Community Gardening Association (ACGA)
1777 East Broad Street
Columbus, OH 43203
(877) ASK-ACGA [275-2242]
Web site: http://www.communitygarden.org
The ACGA supports community gardening projects throughout the
    United States in both rural and urban communities. Its Web site
    has links to teen-friendly resources for community gardening.

American Horticultural Society (AHS)
7931 East Boulevard Drive
Alexandria, VA 22308
Web site: http://www.ahs.org
(703) 768-5700
The American Horticultural Society is an excellent resource
    for species information and planting advice.

City Farmer
Box 74567, Kitsilano RPO
Vancouver, BC V6K 4P4
Canada
(604) 685-5832
Web site: http://www.cityfarmer.info
City Farmer teaches people about urban farming, composting,
    and other environmentally responsible efforts. The Web site
    offers news and stories from Canada and around the world.

Growing Power
5500 W. Silver Spring Drive
Milwaukee, WI 53218
(414) 527-1546
Web site: http://www.growingpower.org
Founded by former professional basketball player Will Allen,
    Growing Power teaches inner-city youth and other commu-
    nity members to become community farmers, assuring them
    a source of fresh, healthy, affordable food and teaching
    them 21st-century career skills such as business manage-
    ment and marketing. The organization has also supplied
    forty thousand children in the Milwaukee Public Schools
    with the food it grows.

National Center for Home Food Preservation (NCHFP)
University of Georgia College of Family and Consumer Sciences
208 Hoke Smith Annex
Athens, GA 30602-4356
Web site: http://nchfp.uga.edu
The NCHFP offers current research and recommendations for all
    kinds of home food preservation methods. Its Web site pro-
    vides recipes, tips, and troubleshooting steps.

National Gardening Association (NGA)
237 Commerce Street, Suite 101
Williston, VT 05495

(802) 863-5251

Web site: http://www.garden.org; http://www.kidsgardening.org

This gardening organization publishes KidsGardening.org, a
    helpful Web site for children and teens who are beginning
    to garden. The site can help young people find grant oppor-
    tunities, awards, resources, and ideas.

U.S. Department of Agriculture (USDA)

National Institute of Food and Agriculture

1400 Independence Avenue SW, Stop 2201

Washington, DC 20250-2201

(202) 720-4423

Web site: http://www.csrees.usda.gov/Extension

The USDA Web site is vast and contains all kinds of information
    for farmers, gardeners, and consumers. This page will help you
    connect to your local cooperative extension office.

WEB SITES

Due to the changing nature of Internet links, Rosen Publishing
has developed an online list of Web sites related to the subject
of this book. This site is updated regularly. Please use this link
to access the list:

http://www.rosenlinks.com/UGFT/Gard

Bartholomew, Mel. *Square Foot Gardening Answer Book*. Minneapolis, MN: Cool Springs Press, 2012.

Bradley, Fern Marshall, Barbara W. Ellis, and Deborah L. Martin. *The Organic Gardener's Handbook of Natural Pest and Disease Control: A Complete Guide to Maintaining a Healthy Garden and Yard the Earth-Friendly Way.* New York, NY: Rodale, 2009.

Carpenter, Novella, and Willow Rosenthal. *The Essential Urban Farmer.* New York, NY: Penguin Books, 2011.

Ellis, David J., and Simon Akeroyd. *New Encyclopedia of Gardening Techniques.* London, England: Mitchell Beazley, 2009.

Elzer-Peters, Katie. *Beginner's Illustrated Guide to Gardening: Techniques to Help You Get Started.* Minneapolis, MN: Cool Springs Press, 2012.

Fox, Thomas J. *Urban Farming: Sustainable City Living in Your Backyard, in Your Community, and in the World.* Irvine, CA: Hobby Farm Press/BowTie Press, 2011.

Green, Doug. *Guide to Canadian Vegetable Gardening*. Minneapolis, MN: Cool Springs Press, 2009.

Green, Jen. *A Teen Guide to Eco-Gardening, Food, and Cooking* (Eco Guides). Chicago, IL: Capstone Heinemann Library, 2013.

Lewis, Barbara A. *The Kid's Guide to Social Action: How to Solve the Social Problems You Choose—and Turn Creative Thinking into Positive Action.* Rev., expanded, updated ed. Minneapolis, MN: Free Spirit Publishing, 2004.

Nardozzi, Charlie. *The Ultimate Gardener: The Best Experts' Advice for Cultivating a Magnificent Garden, with Photos and Stories.* Deerfield Beach, FL: Health Communications, 2009.

Olson, Diane. *A Nature Lover's Almanac: Kinky Bugs, Stealthy Critters, Prosperous Plants & Celestial Wonders.* Layton, UT: Gibbs Smith, 2012.

Pennington, Amy. *Apartment Gardening: Plants, Projects, and Recipes for Growing Food in Your Urban Home.* Seattle, WA: Sasquatch Books, 2011.

Rankin, Kenrya. *Start It Up: The Complete Teen Business Guide to Turning Your Passions into Pay.* San Francisco, CA: Zest Books, 2011.

Richardson, Fern. *Small-Space Container Gardens: Transform Your Balcony, Porch, or Patio with Fruits, Flowers, Foliage & Herbs.* Portland, OR: Timber Press, 2012.

Silverstein, Clara. *A White House Garden Cookbook: Healthy Ideas from the First Family for Your Family.* New York, NY: Red Rock Press, 2010.

Smith, Charles W. G. *The Beginner's Guide to Edible Herbs: 26 Herbs Everyone Should Grow & Enjoy.* North Adams, MA: Storey Publishing, 2010.

Tornio, Stacy. *Project Garden: A Month-by-Month Guide to Planting, Growing, and Enjoying All Your Backyard Has to Offer.* Avon, MA: Adams Media, 2012.

Whittingham, Jo. *Garden Rescue: First Aid for Plants and Flowers.* New York, NY: DK Publishing, 2013.

BIBLIOGRAPHY

Agricultural Research Service, U.S. Department of Agriculture. "USDA Plant Hardiness Zone Map." 2012. Retrieved February 23, 2013 (http://www.ahs.org).

American Horticultural Society. "AHS Plant Heat Zone Map." 2012. Retrieved February 23, 2013 (http://www.ahs.org).

Ayer, Kevin, and Cindy A. Littlefield. *The Vegetable Gardener's Book of Building Projects.* North Adams, MA: Storey Publishing, 2010.

Capalbo, Danielle. "Teen Initiates Community Garden at Trackside." *Wilton Villager*, April 15, 2011. Retrieved February 28, 2013 (http://www.thehour.com).

Cohen, Whitney, and John Fisher. *The Book of Gardening Projects for Kids: 101 Ways to Get Kids Outside, Dirty, and Having Fun.* Portland, OR: Timber Press, 2012.

Coleman-Jensen, Alisha, Mark Nord, Margaret Andrews, and Steven Carlson. "ERS Report Summary: Household Food Security in the United States in 2011." Economic Research Service, U.S. Department of Agriculture, September 2012. Retrieved March 1, 2013 (http://www.ers.usda.gov).

Coupland, Bob. "Teens Dig into Community Garden." *Tribune Chronicle*, May 7, 2010. Retrieved February 28, 2013 (http://www.tribtoday.com).

Gianfrancesco, Richard. *How to Grow Food: A Step-by-Step Guide to Growing All Kinds of Fruits, Vegetables, Salads, and More.* Buffalo, NY: Firefly Books, 2011.

Johnson, Samantha, and Daniel Johnson. *The Beginner's Guide to Vegetable Gardening.* Minneapolis, MN: Voyageur Press, 2013.

Martin, Heide. "Rebel Tomato." American Community Gardening Association, 2007. Retrieved February 28, 2013 (http://www .communitygarden.org/rebeltomato/).

Moss-Sprague, Mary. *Stand Up and Garden.* Woodstock, VT: Countryman Press, 2012.

Murphy, Donna M., and Angela Williams Duea. *The Complete Guide to Growing Windowsill Plants.* Ocala, FL: Atlantic Publishing Group, 2011.

Pyenson, Andrea. "Boston Teens Grow Green." *Edible Boston,* February 27, 2013. Retrieved March 1, 2013 (http:// edibleboston.com).

Ray, Janisse. *The Seed Underground: A Growing Revolution to Save Food.* White River Junction, VT: Chelsea Green Publishing, 2012.

Smith, Jeremy N. *Growing a Garden City.* New York, NY: Skyhorse Publishing, 2010.

Stewart, Keith. *Storey's Guide to Growing Organic Vegetables & Herbs for Market.* North Adams, MA: Storey Publishing, 2013.

Taylor, Lisa. *Your Farm in the City: An Urban Dweller's Guide to Growing Food and Raising Livestock.* New York, NY: Black Dog & Leventhal Publishers, 2011.

Urban Harvest Community Gardens Program. "Start a Community Garden." UrbanHarvest.org. Retrieved March 2, 2013 (http:// www.urbanharvest.org).

INDEX

ABOUT THE AUTHOR

Susan Burns Chong, LMSW, has worked with teens for almost twenty years. A lifelong enthusiastic gardener, she has grown vegetables and herbs in community gardens with young people in New Jersey, Minnesota, and Maine. She is currently project coordinator at a special education and alternative middle and high school in Maine at which students grow their own food and prepare lunches for the school campus. In the summer, she is most often seen in the garden, watering plants, battling weeds, or harvesting fresh food with her family.

PHOTO CREDITS

Cover © iStockphoto.com/Jani Bryson; pp. 5, 15, 19, 25 © AP Images; p. 8 Universal Images Group/Getty Images; p. 10 Boston Globe/Getty Images; pp. 12, 18, 24 iStockphoto/Thinkstock; p. 22 USDA Plant Hardiness Zone Map, 2012, ARS, USDA; p. 33 Jake Wyman/The Image Bank/Getty Images; p. 34 Chris Price/E+/Getty Images; p. 36 Chris Hondros/Getty Images; p. 40 © Syracuse Newspapers/E M Blalock/The Image Works; p. 42 The Washington Post/Getty Images; p. 43 Michael Underwood/Getty Images; p. 46 Hyoung Chang/Denver Post/Getty Images; p. 48 Chicago Tribune/McClatchy-Tribune/Getty Images; p. 50 Harrison Smith/Toronto Star/Getty Images; cover and interior pages (cityscape silhouette) © iStockphoto.com/blackred; cover, p. 1 (roots silhouette) © iStockphoto.com/John Woodcock; back cover (plants silhouette) © iStockphoto.com/Mlenny; interior pages (dirt) © iStockphoto.com/wragg.

Designer: Nicole Russo; Editor: Andrea Sclarow Paskoff; Photo Researcher: Amy Feinberg